D1542018

SEVEN DAYS
THAT CHANGED
THE WORLD

SEVEN DAYS
THAT CHANGED
THE WORLD

Lenten Sermons Based
upon the Events of
the Last Week in
the Life of Jesus

WALLACE T. VIETS

ABINGDON PRESS
New York • Nashville

SEVEN DAYS THAT CHANGED THE WORLD

Copyright © 1962 by Abingdon Press

Library of Congress Catalog Card Number: 62-8109

SET UP, PRINTED, AND BOUND BY THE
PARTHENON PRESS, AT NASHVILLE,
TENNESSEE, UNITED STATES OF AMERICA

To

Evelyn

who has heard more of my preaching
than anyone else and whose steadfast
loyalty and creatively critical comments are ever designed to improve
the proclamation of the truth in love

Preface

THE SEVEN GREATEST DAYS IN HISTORY ARE FASCINAT-
ing, not only as individual portions of the gospel,
but as parts of an integrated whole. What started
many years ago as a series of Lenten Bible-study
topics has developed into this series of Lenten
sermons.

To those who have urged that these be printed,
I am grateful for their confidence. To the late
Halford E. Luccock and John C. Schroeder, teachers
of preachers extraordinary, I owe thanks for stimu-
lation in the homiletic arts. To my parents and the
congregations who awakened and nurtured love
for the things of God, I shall always be in debt.

Ideas and impressions come from so many different sources that one can never hope to acknowledge
them all. Careful attempt has been made to give

credit wherever possible. I would thank those who transcribed the original tape recordings of these sermons and helped in the editing.

This series of sermons was preached in part from the pulpit of Christ Church, Methodist, Glens Falls, New York, and, in substantially its present form, from the pulpit of the First Methodist Church of New Haven, Connecticut. The encouragement of members of these congregations is gratefully acknowledged.

WALLACE T. VIETS

Contents

9

Introduction

OVER ONE THIRD OF ALL THE MATERIAL IN THE gospel accounts of the life of Jesus deals with the events of the last week of his earthly life. In the Revised Standard Version of the New Testament, these four accounts occupy about 250 pages. Of these, eighty-five contain the teachings and happenings beginning with the triumphal entry into Jerusalem and ending with the post-Resurrection appearances. The individual accounts vary all the way from about one quarter of the total text in the Gospel according to Luke to one half of the total in the Gospel according to John.

This emphasis indicates clearly that, in the view of the early church, the most important part of the revelation of God in Jesus Christ was reflected in what took place in this last week. It is not possible to harmonize all the material completely, but it is possible to group it approximately and to consider

11

the biblical accounts day by day. This series of sermons is based for the most part on the account of the last week as recorded by Luke. It has been necessary to make some internal adjustments as Luke's material is not clearly divided by days. For example, there is no separation in Luke between the triumphal entry and the cleansing of the Temple. Traditionally, however, it has been assumed (and is so indicated in the other two Synoptics) that these two events did not take place on the same day.

For ease in following the days of the week, the names of the days which we habitually use have been assigned to each of the days from Palm Sunday through Easter Day. The events and the days of the week are grouped for this series as follows:

Palm Sunday—The triumphal entry as recorded in Luke 19:28-40.

Monday—Weeping over the city and cleansing the Temple as recorded in Luke 19:41-48.

Tuesday—The didactic discourses as recorded in Luke 20 and 21.

Wednesday—The retirement at Bethany, of which there is no record in Luke. However, in both Mark and Matthew, there appears at this point the account of the anointing at the home of Simon of Bethany.

Maundy Thursday—The Last Supper and the Garden of Gethsemane as recorded in Luke 22:7-30, and 39-46.

Good Friday—The trials and the Crucifixion as recorded in Luke 22 and 23.

Saturday—There is no account of any events between the removal of the body from the cross, the laying of the body in the tomb of Joseph of Arimathea, the sealing of the tomb as recorded in Matthew, and the events of the first day of the week. The only reference in Luke reads: "On the sabbath they rested according to the commandment."

Easter Day—The Resurrection and appearances as recorded in Luke 23 and 24.

PALM SUNDAY

The Day of Temporary Triumph

Scripture Lesson: **Luke 19:28-40**

PALM SUNDAY IS A DAY OF GREAT JOY, BUT IT IS ALSO A puzzle. There is an enigma about Palm Sunday. What does it mean? Is it an end or a beginning? Is it a climax or a commencement? Or is it a point of division between two parts of the ministry and witness of Jesus?

Note the phrase in the New Testament lesson: "[They] began to sing aloud the praises of God for all the things they had seen" (N.E.B.). The enigma is that apparently the same people who sang praises for what he had done on Palm Sunday also shouted "Crucify him!" for what they had refused to do in following him. Yes, Palm Sunday is something of a puzzle; the meaning is not entirely clear. Is it a triumph or a tragedy; is it a symbol of success or of failure?

The answer to that rhetorical question is anticipated by calling Palm Sunday the day of *temporary* triumph. This is the key to understanding the day. There is no need to refuse to celebrate the day, but we should recognize the celebration not as an end in itself, but as a prelude to something greater. It is not a group of people hailing Jesus at the end of his ministry. It is a group of people, unfortunately, responding to only part of his witness —not fully understanding the totality of witness— giving a spontaneous expression of their feeling of joy. They did not fully understand until the week had been completed. Perhaps they never fully understood. This is the continuing problem, not only of Palm Sunday, but of all of Holy Week. It marks the end of that part of Jesus' ministry which received spontaneous approval from the people who heard him gladly, who flocked around him because of the healing and the miracles, who responded to the great things he had done. It marks the beginning of that part of the ministry where Jesus delved so much deeper that the people left him and forsook him. This deeper witness culminated in the eternal triumph of Easter.

As we sing our hymns of praise on Palm Sunday, there are three things in the New Testament lesson to call to mind: the symbolism of the entry itself; the meaning of applause in general as well as spontaneously expressed approval; and the curious exchange of comments between the Pharisees and Jesus.

I

Consider the symbolic significance of Jesus' manner of entry into the city. Instead of riding a horse, the symbol of kingly power, or even a camel, a much more dignified animal, Jesus came simply, riding a donkey—a beast of burden. To borrow, without irreverence, from television westerns, instead of storming into town on a horse, six-shooters blazing, he came in riding a little burro, the beast of burden usually reserved for the simpleton. How did this fit in with the expected Messiah? Should not the Messiah be a symbol of righteousness; and should he not use all means to achieve that righteousness? Instead he came riding a colt upon which "no one has ever yet sat." He came not as a man of war, about to use force; he came as a man of peace, in deep humility.

His steed was obtained in a rather peculiar way. Some commentators have suggested that the phrase used by the disciples of Jesus in speaking to the donkey's owner may have been a prearranged password: "The Lord has need of it." Others suggest that the obtaining of the animal is another example of clairvoyance on the part of Jesus, coupled with response to need by the owner. Whichever interpretation you prefer, consider the verbal exchange: "What are you doing with this donkey?" "The Lord has need of it." Isn't it surprising that the owner raised no objection? He might well have replied: "Well, that's too bad. It's mine and I need it, too!"

Throughout our lives, there come similar requests—some prearranged, some without warning. These are requests for talents, time, consecrated ability. "The Lord has need of it." Is your answer, "But I need it more"? Whether clairvoyance or a password, this *is* the password to full and abundant life. When the call "The Lord has need of it" comes, the response can be the entrance into significant, full, and abundant experience.

II

After the donkey was obtained, there came the enthusiasm of the disciples. The word "disciple" here refers not to the twelve, nor even to the seventy. Presumably it refers to the multitudes and to those who may not have known Jesus before. They were swept along on a wave of contagious emotion.

How easy it is to pick up a mob on a wave of emotion. But this emotion was very temporary, because it was not undergirded by basic understanding. We can be pretty certain that many of the same people who shouted "Hosanna!" also shouted "Crucify!" Do we? Do we praise with our lips, but repudiate in our lives? This is the soul-searching question of Palm Sunday. Do we, beneath and beyond the songs of praise, the spontaneous expressions of our lips, likewise participate in the Good Friday experience?

Turn the coin over. The plaudits of the crowd, applause and approval with our lips are always rather temporary, are they not? Can they be a firm basis for ultimate decision? Is it not amazing in our day to see the ease with which we assume that majority opinion determines value? The details of the procedure by which the value of television programs is measured are complicated, but it has something to do with the number of sets tuned in to a given program at a given time. The program with the most watchers is the best program. What an incredible idea! How does one ever improve?

In contrast, note that every advance in human experience has come as the conviction of a minority or a single person who was in touch with basic and ultimate reality. We know to our sorrow that moral law does not depend upon majority opinion, any more than physical law does. A life that is based only upon applause, the plaudits of the crowd, has no foundation, because this approval is not lasting. It changes. The person who bases his life on a desire to please everyone discovers first of all that this is impossible, because people have conflicting and contradictory desires. He who tries ends up pleasing neither everyone, nor himself, nor God. *Vox populi* non *est vox Dei.* The voice of the people is *not* the voice of God, unless the voice of the people has first been turned over to God, and those who speak have committed themselves to him. One wonders if those who shouted on that first Palm Sunday understood.

There is value in what they said, however, as a starting point. There is a curious correlation between Luke's account of what the people shouted and the song of the angels at the birth of Jesus. Have you ever noted it? Luke, writing presumably for Greeks and Gentiles, did not use the word "hosanna." His readers might not have understood it. Instead, he used the phrase, "Blessed be the King who comes in the name of the Lord! Peace in heaven and glory in the highest!" Remember what the angels sang at Jesus' birth, according to Luke: "Glory to God in the highest, and on earth, peace!" (2:14). Glory and peace—peace and glory. There can never be peace among men or within men apart from glory to God. Is this not the teaching of the birth story as Luke has it and the teaching of Palm Sunday as well?

Someone has paraphrased the above statement: "Peace is prepared by God in heaven to be bestowed on men,—may He who dwells on high be glorified!" [1] Our world seeks for peace, we say. Mankind has always sought for peace, but we must learn that peace is not the absence of war; it is something more, something positive. It involves reconciliation. It involves that process which knows that the only way to destroy an enemy is by transforming him

[1] B. S. Easton, *The Gospel According to St. Luke* (New York: Charles Scribner's Sons, 1926), p. 286.

into a friend. The people expected something quite different from a Messiah. Do we?

III

Note, now, that curious rebuke of the Pharisees, those leaders of the religious life of their people. "Teacher, rebuke your disciples." *Tell this motley crowd to be quiet. This is an unseemly demonstration. Tell them to calm down.* Jesus, replying in oriental hyperbole, said, "I tell you, if these were silent, the very stones would cry out." This is not to be taken literally, for certainly Jesus did not mean that music and words would come from stones. He is saying that the revelation of truth that he has come to bring is written into the very fabric of the universe. Even if we cannot grasp it or refuse to accept it from him, it will demonstrate itself. The nature of God that he has revealed is not something new in creation, though it is new in the understanding of mankind. It is written in the fabric of the universe. The revolution that takes place is the revolution within the hearts of men.

When Nikita Khrushchev visited the United States in September, 1959, he was reported as having said that he and Jesus Christ have a great deal in common. Mr. K. suggested that he agrees with much of what Jesus said. This need not concern us. The truth of Jesus' statements do not depend upon Khrushchev's approval or lack of it. However, Mr. K. made one important proviso. He said, in effect: "The one thing where Jesus is all wrong is where he talks about sacrificial love or where he says that 'if a man smite thee on the one cheek, turn to him the other also.'" Khrushchev said: "If a man strikes me on one cheek, I'll hit him back on the other one and knock his head off!" He, as have so many, has missed completely the central truth of the Christian gospel: that it is in self-sacrificing love, in self-givingness—and only in this way—that peace can come. A world that is teetering on the edge of terror, with tremendous powers for destruction held in uneasy rein, is not at peace. This may be—and thanks be to God, it is at this point—the absence of *overt* conflict, but this is *not* peace.

When John Wesley was rebuked for the preaching that he was doing, he said to his bishop, "The church has kept silent and now the stones have cried out." There are examples of this happening in every age. One of the tragedies in South Africa is that the former premier, Daniel Malan, who instituted the strict regime of subjugation which we see today in that unhappy land, was one of the ruling group in the Christian church of South Africa. In our own land, so often it has been the sports teams, the labor unions, the Supreme Court rulings which have led while the churches have temporized with our greatest social evil. Did you note with shame the report of the Civil Rights Commission which indicated that there is discrimination based on race, relgion, or national origin in housing, in employment, and in public accommodations, not just in nine or eleven southern states, nor even just in twenty-five states but in fifty states of this union? The discrimination is not in equal measure in all parts of the country, but in every state there are indications that we still have not come to the point of recognizing that all human creatures are of equal worth in the sight of the heavenly Father. When the proclamation of brotherhood is rebuked, the facts of history—the very stones—cry out.

There is something monumentally ironic about the statement that appeared in a book by Eve Curie, the daughter of Marie and Pierre, who discovered radium and started the whole process leading to the release of atomic energy. In a book published in 1943, two years B.A.B. (before atom bomb), written while the author was sitting on a hill overlooking Jerusalem, these words were addressed to Jesus:

> You told us to be kind and forgiving, but for twenty solid centuries, wretched, incorrigible men have gone on being merciless, full of violence and of hatred. Religious men and atheists alike have lived and ruled in a non-Christian way—and look at us now: we've never been in a worse mess! [2]

In a book entitled *By an Unknown Disciple* there is a scene in which Jesus is talking to the

---

[2] Eve Curie, *Journey Among Warriors* (New York: Doubleday, Doran and Co., Inc., 1943), p. 96.

23

disciples as they are looking over the city. Judas is speaking:

"Seeing the power you have over the people, I have told them you will end the oppression."

"By driving forth the oppressors?" asked Jesus.

"Yes," cried Judas, "by thrusting them into the sea. By breaking their Empire in pieces, and humbling them so that they whisper out of the dust."

When Judas finished, Jesus rose and from the height on which we stood, he looked over the plain below, . . . with its towns, its crops and woods. . . . He seemed to withdraw into himself as if to gather strength, and then he turned again to Judas, and his face was full of graciousness, like one of the holy angels.

"Will that end oppression?" he asked, and waited for a reply.

None came, for with the question, we all, even Judas, fell silent.[3]

IV

Palm Sunday marks the beginning of the great drama of redemption. It marks the beginning of that experience which shows the depth of the love of God for us. It marks the beginning of the expression of the idea that the only way in which salvation—however you define the term—can come is through willing sacrifice, through the willingness to give.

[3] *By an Unknown Disciple* (New York: George H. Doran, 1919), pp. 75 ff. Used by permission of Harper & Brothers.

Palm Sunday is a glorious day; it should not be taken from the calendar. It should be emphasized that it is not an end in itself, but rather a beginning. It can mark a beginning for each one of us. For

> I watched the Captains
>> A-riding, riding
>> Down the years;
> The men of mystic grip
>> Of soul, a-riding
> Between a hedge of spears.
>
> I saw their banners
>> A-floating, floating
>> Over all,
> Till each of them had passed,
>> And Christ came riding
> A donkey lean and small.
>
> I watched the Captains
>> A-turning, staring,
>> Proud and set,
> At Christ a-riding there—
>> So calmly riding
> The Road men can't forget.
>
> I watched the Captains
>> Dismounting, waiting—
>> None now led—
> The Captains bowing low!
> The Caesars waiting!
> While Christ rode on ahead.[4]

[4] Arthur Macdougall, Jr., "The Captains of the Years." From *Far Enough for All the Years.* Used by permission of the author.

MONDAY

The Day of Emotion

Scripture Lesson: Luke 19:41-48

HOW DO YOU FACE DISAPPOINTMENT AND FRUSTRA-
tion? What is your reaction in the face of something
you consider to be wrong? Do you face it with tears
or with temper? With cries of anguish or shouts of
anger? With weeping or with wrath? It is interesting to note as we read accounts of the life of Jesus,
that he used both. This may surprise us at first, but
then we see that he didn't stop with either!

In considering the events which took place during the last week on the day corresponding to Monday, note, in Luke's account, considerable emotion
being expressed by Jesus. Examine his weeping and
his wrath—his anguish and his anger—his tears
and his temper. Then consider the sequel.

26

I

The events of Monday began with a very strange scene. Jesus and his disciples had traveled down from Galilee, the northern part of Palestine. We say "traveled down" because he came south. The good Jew, however, would always say, if his destination were Jerusalem, no matter where one starts, he is traveling "up." At any rate, Jesus and his companions had come to Jerusalem to join in the Passover. This festival was the combination of the ultimate in religious expression and the ultimate in patriotic expression. Apparently, the group discovered there was no place to stay in the city; so they went back to stay with friends in the suburb of Bethany. The morning following the triumphal entry, Jesus came back into the city. As he came up over the rise in the ground and saw the city, he stopped and wept.

He wept over the city—this symbol of the greatness of his people, this embodiment of the hopes for the future of his people, this great city whose name means "city of peace." What a monumental irony that this city, which today is torn by strife and dissensions, should be called the "city of peace." Perhaps there is good reason for weeping! The weeping was accompanied by words expressing his sorrow. In his mind may well have been the lament uttered earlier in Luke's account: "O Jerusalem, Jerusalem, killing the prophets and stoning those who are sent to you!" (13:34.) To these he added: "Would that

27

even today you knew the things that make for peace!" *Oh, if only you knew, even at this eleventh hour, on what your peace depends!* "But now they are hid from your eyes. For the days shall come upon you, when your enemies will cast up a bank about you and surround you, and hem you in on every side, and dash you to the ground, you and your children within you, and they will not leave one stone upon another in you; because you did not know the time of your visitation." (19:43-44.) *You did not know when God himself was visiting you.*

Whether the writer of this account was writing after the fall of Jersualem or only doing some good second guessing is beside the point. The basic meaning of this episode is that all human projects that do not take into consideration the purpose of God are doomned to destruction. So, Jesus wept.

Note that a person weeps only if he feels deeply about something. We don't cry about things that mean nothing. Indeed, one's capacity to weep and feel deeply is a direct indication of the depth of his spirit and the extent of his sensitivity. As we look around the world today, there are many things about which we might weep. Consider a few of them.

Do you recall Nevil Shute's *On the Beach?*[1] In this novel, set in the year 1964 in Australia, we are presented with the last days of life on earth follow-

[1] (New York: William Morrow and Co., Inc., 1957.)

ing an accidentally started nuclear war which so poisoned the atmosphere that all living creatures were doomed. What monumental irony! It was an accident that the human race committed suicide.

You may remember, from the movie based on the book, one scene in the submarine where the officers, some of the crew, and the English scientist, Julian, are discussing the war and how it started. The sailors blame Julian and the other scientists— after all, it was the scientists who discovered atomic energy, wasn't it? Julian replies, "Who would have thought that human beings would be stupid enough to blow themselves off the face of the earth?" "But when did it all start?" asks an officer. "When did it start?" Julian replies. "The war started when people accepted the idiotic idea that peace could be maintained by arranging to defend themselves with weapons they couldn't possibly use without committing suicide."

The most interesting part of this is that there is no clergyman in it, no church or reference to religion, except, in the movie version, in the scene where the Salvation Army is holding forth beneath a banner reading, "There Is Still Time, Brother." Although the scene is rather pathetic, it is obvious that this is not basic to the picture.

My first reaction to the absence of any mention of religious values is a negative one. But this absence may reflect far deeper meaning. Perhaps it symbolizes the fact that when God and the church are put either out of or on the periphery of our lives, then destruction and the end of life are upon us. Whether this was intended or not, there is this message in the film.

When did it start? It starts even before man accepts the idiotic idea to which Julian referred. It starts whenever man thinks he can get along without God!

Has it started?

Consider another impression. Whenever a film built around a "religious" or "biblical" theme appears, a minister is sure to be asked questions about it. Do you remember *Solomon and Sheba?* In the issue of *Newsweek* in which this film was reviewed there appeared two quotations from different publicity media. Under the title ". . . But Whose Sheba?" the writer has these comments:

> In an ad for a big denominational semimonthly, here is what one hand wrote: "Attention religious instructors. Bring the Biblical world of Solomon and Sheba to exciting life in your classroom! Informative Bible-kit Available Free."
>
> For a secular media, UA's other hand made a quite different pitch: ". . . The central figure in the dance is Gina Lollobrigida. In her navel is a crescent-shaped ruby, which gleams and glitters while she performs the orgiastic dance which ends in her seduction of Solomon." [2]

The *Newsweek* writer then quotes from an edi-

[2] *Newsweek,* March 14, 1960, p. 94. Used by permission.

torial in the *Christian Herald:* "This is for Sunday schools?"

Might we not weep in the face of this zeal for the dollar, however obtained, from both sides of the street? Appeal to bogus religious values, appeal to the baser instincts—any appeal is justified if it pays off in profits! This is cause for weeping.

In the capital of our great land, looked to for leadership by all the peoples of the earth, we can see the various parliamentary devices by which the representatives of a small fraction of this country thwart the right of every citizen to equal opportunity. During the early weeks of 1960 there was a filibuster in the Senate of the United States in opposition to certain civil rights legislation. The sixteen senators from the eight states manning the filibuster represented states with a total population of 19,715,000 according to the census then in effect, the one of 1950. Also, according to that census, 6,118,000 of the population of those eight states were Negroes, none of whom was being represented by the senators involved! In most cases those 6,000,000 Negroes had not been allowed to vote for their senators; and even if they had been, it is not reasonable to suppose that the opposition to civil rights legislation by the senators represented the Negroes' point of view! It may be, then, that these sixteen senators represented the point of view of the other 13,597,000 residents. These total less than 9 per cent of the total population of the country on the basis of the 1950 census. Our nation, therefore, presented to the world the spectacle of the representatives of less than 9 per cent of the population controlling the legislative process at that particular time and blocking action in the one area which is more important, in the eyes of the uncommitted, nonwhite population of the world, than any other. Is this democracy? Is it very convincing to go to the rest of the world and say, "This is the way you should govern yourselves"? Who is un-American, anyway? This is cause for weeping.

There are so many other instances of matters over which our first reaction is frustrated tears. We can multiply the illustrations of injustice and blindness which prevent the realization of true peace and brotherhood. Our national propensity for being against so much without being for those great truths we should share with all the world is cause for weeping—as is the incredible disproportion between the amount spent every year by our nation in developing methods of destruction as compared with the amount we spend exploring ways of making peace.

However, though tears, anguish, and weeping reflect an ability to feel deeply, they have very little positive value. Jesus wept over the city, yes. But he did not stop with weeping. He went down off the hill into the city. He went into the temple where he found instances of exploitation of the people. You remember what he did.

II

The late Dean Tertius Van Dyke of the Hartford Theological Seminary once said, "Sometimes I think that the capacity for getting angry is a real qualification for the Christian ministry." To paraphrase that statement: "Sometimes the capacity for getting angry is a real qualification for Christian life." Jesus became morally indignant, but he didn't stop with his indignation. Remember particularly what he became angry *about*. He did *not* become angry because he had been thwarted or because something he wanted did not come to pass or because something was taken away from him. He became angry when children of God were exploited; when men were casual about holy things; when God's purpose was frustrated. In his moral indignation in the Temple, he cleansed it. But note, the cleansing was only temporary. Here again is monumental irony.

The episode of the cleansing of the Temple is not a justification for the indiscriminate use of force. It is ridiculous to assume that one man, depending entirely upon physical force, could have cleared that courtyard. It is probable that the moral indignation of this man, of this Son of God, struck a fire in the consciences of the people there and they left—but only temporarily. The next day they were back, for their practice continued—the changing of money for the payment of the Temple tax, the selling of animals for sacrificial purposes.

What, then, is the use of wrath and anger? It represents energy; it represents response to something felt deeply. Only those who feel deeply become angry. A Casper Milquetoast is seldom, if ever, angry. But there are two kinds of anger. One proceeds from personal frustration, and is not Christian. The other kind proceeds from consciousness of the frustration of God. This anger characterized Elijah, Amos, Isaiah, Micah, Jeremiah, Paul, Martin Luther. It characterized a gaunt, homely young man who, after riding down the Mississippi on a flatboat and standing in a market place in New Orleans and watching, for the first time, human beings bought and sold as cattle, said, "If I ever get a chance, I'll hit this thing and I'll hit it hard." [3] Abraham Lincoln did hit it hard in 1863 when he penned the Emancipation Proclamation.

This kind of anger may release energy which can be used for constructive purposes, but it has to be directed. It cannot be like the anger of the hunter who, waking up at night to the sound of a buzzing fly, grabbed his shotgun and fired at the side of the tent. He killed the fly, but he didn't leave much of the tent standing! The anger that expresses itself in just one big explosion—one big spectacle—is useless. Steam power is valuable, but steam pressure

[3] From *The Story-Life of Lincoln*, ed. Wayne Whipple.

that builds up with no place to go causes a destructive explosion. Power must be directed.

Anger by itself always fails, unless the energy is transmuted. Hear the Proverbs: "The fool rageth, and is confident" (14:16, K.J.V.). Or hear James: "The anger of man does not work the righteousness of God" (1:20).

III

After tears and anger, then what? Jesus didn't stop with weeping, anguish and tears—with wrath, anger, and temper. His sorrowful wrath became self-sacrificing witness. He who wept over Jerusalem and cleansed the Temple in moral indignation gave himself on the cross later in the week.

Ask yourselves, then, what makes you angry and what makes you sorrowful. Is it personal frustration or the frustration of God's purpose of good for all mankind? What are you doing about it?

On the front of a leaflet for use on Red Cross Sunday there appeared the following statement:

Every day the Lord gives each of us opportunities for serving others. The service may be of great magnitude, or so small as to pass almost unrecognized by finite eyes; but in His sight, there is no distinction between the great and the small, and every service done with love of the Lord and our fellow man receives Divine recognition. All those who serve . . . are thrice blessed. They have the assurance that they are helping their neighbors; they are building better communities; and from the deep sense of personal satisfaction which comes to them, they know that truly good things happen to those who serve.

How true this is of all the Christian life.

In his Corinthian correspondence, Paul makes this categorical statement: "Be sure that nothing you do for him is ever lost or ever wasted" (I Cor. 15:58, Phillips).

One of the most spirited hymns we have is "Lead On, O King Eternal." It sounds, as we sing it, as though it extols muscular vitality and energetic activity. But note the last two lines of the second stanza:

> For not with swords loud clashing,
> Nor roll of stirring drums;
> With *deeds of love and mercy*,
> The heav'nly kingdom comes.

What a privilege for each one of us to be a part of this great host that works through deeds of love and mercy; that has the capacity to cry, to feel deeply; that has the conviction to respond energetically by directing this sensitivity and energy into creative channels, through self-sacrificing witness, in emulation of him who gave himself for us.

TUESDAY

The Day of Creative Controversy

Scripture Lesson:
Selections from Luke 20 and 21

HOW DOES ONE DISCOVER TRUTH? HOW DOES ONE TEST truth? How does one go about determining, between two propositions, which is true and which is false? Knowledge, data, facts, information, understanding come from four different sources. Certain things are learned by experience. Certain things are learned through the action of our minds, the operation of our reason. Certain things are self-evident and come as revelation. Certain things come to us with the authority of tradition as a part of the inherited experience from those who have gone before. All information partakes, to a greater or lesser degree, of all four of these aspects.

The question still remains, however, in a changing social situation: "How do we decide which of two or three propositions or procedures for action is true?" This question seemed uppermost in Jesus' mind on this day.

Following the triumphal entry and the cleansing of the Temple, Jesus returned the following day to the Temple courtyard and offered to answer any questions anyone might bring to him. He sat talking with his disciples and with anyone else who cared to converse with him. No lines of inquiry were eliminated—"no holds were barred"—in this open-forum search for truth. He was acting in the spirit of the rabbis of his people. He was recognizing the importance of controversy in arriving at truth—controversy neither bitter, cynical, nor contentious, but creative. This day corresponding to Tuesday was not just a day of controversy, but was a day of *creative* controversy. Consider, then, the need in our day for creative controversy as a method for determining truth and then consider three specific points that Jesus made that day.

I

There is a difference between argument and discussion. Argument may well be self-defeating, for argument for its own sake is a competitive activity, engaged in by opponents, each of whom is anxious to win. Discussion is a consideration in open forum of possibly conflicting ideas or propositions, with a view to discovering the truth that will emerge from the clash of these ideas. The rabbis used this method, as did Jesus. Much of our society is based upon the conscious or unconscious use of this method.

Surely in science this is the process used. A scientist will discover what he thinks to be a true interpretation and will phrase it in terms of a hypothesis which he propounds to the world. He then invites all the rest of the world to attack his proposition. He knows that if his hypothesis is true, it will withstand all attack. If it is not true, it does not deserve to stand and the attack upon it will produce more profound truth. Several different theories of the nature of light have been advanced in this century. They were replaced as new truth was discovered, and now there is something called the "quantum corpuscular" theory which has virtually replaced the old "ether-wave" theory. The new understanding and the new glimpse of truth has grown not from individuals who pledged themselves to maintain to the death a particular theory whether or not observable facts supported it. Rather, a proposition was set, examined, and replaced by another hypothesis as a result of creative controversy.

Much of our judicial process is based upon this same idea. Each side attempts to state its case as completely and as accurately as possible, believing then, that in the free interchange, the truth will emerge. This process should also be operative in the social realm, within the church, and within the context of the social problems that surround us on every side, nationally and internationally.

There are dangers in engaging in controversy, particularly if it is engaged in merely for its own sake, or if it is engaged in only out of a contentious feeling. There is danger in overplaying one idea, in riding a single hobbyhorse. There once was a country fiddler who could play only one tune—a tune out of the Spanish-American War—"There'll Be a Hot Time in the Old Town Tonight." He played it well. He could play it in several keys and at several tempos. He played it appropriately at family gatherings in the small rural town, and at weddings and square dances he could always be counted upon for "There'll Be a Hot Time in the Old Town Tonight." He ran into some difficulty, however, when he was invited one night to play at a wake!

Yes, there is danger in overplaying one idea. There is danger inherent in holding to an inflexible opinion. One of the popular fallacies of our day is that every man has a right to his own opinion. Every man does *not* have the right to his own opinion *in the face of contradictory evidence,* nor does any man have a right to his own opinion, *untested.* Everyone has the obligation to develop his own opinions on the basis of the best information he can manage, but he also has an obligation to test those opinions constantly.

Another danger we face is our fear to stand up and

be counted. The fear of being different is a terrible thing, particularly in a nation whose glory has come from the capacity that developed the melting pot—the capacity to take different ideas and different interpretations and in the interplay, to come up with something greater than the sum of the parts. There is danger when we are fearful of standing up, being counted, and speaking out and, instead, seek refuge in expressing ideas anonymously or not at all.

A wonderful story about anonymous letters comes from the life of Henry Ward Beecher. In addition to being a great preacher, he was a public figure in Brooklyn and throughout the nation. As is the case with many public figures, he received his share of anonymous letters. One day he received an envelope in the mail containing a sheet of paper on which was written in large letters the single word, "fool." The next Sunday in his pulpit, he described this letter and said, "During my lifetime I have received many letters from people who forgot to sign their names. But this is the first time that anyone ever signed his name and forgot to write the letter!" [1] That's just about it, isn't it? This is the perfect description of the person who is afraid to stand and be counted and support his ideas.

Jesus was asked, *By what authority do you do what you do? Who has given you the right; who has*

[1] John Homer Miller, *Take a Second Look at Yourself* (Nashville: Abingdon Press, 1950), pp. 77-78

commissioned you? He didn't say, "Well, I'm sent from God," or "I have special privilege or special qualifications," or something of that sort. His specific answer will be considered later. Note, here, however, that the whole impact of his ministry seems to say, "Things are not true because I say so. I say them because I believe them to be true." This is fundamental.

It was Woodrow Wilson who suggested, "I have always been among those who believe that the greatest freedom of speech was the greatest safety, because if a man is a fool, the best thing to do is to encourage him to advertise the fact by speaking." It was Woodrow Wilson who held to the ideal in international relations of open covenants, openly arrived at. Our ideal should be open decisions, openly arrived at, through free and open discussions.

Yes, creative, open controversy is needed. Jesus engaged in it and recognized its value. Consider now just three of the many issues raised on that Tuesday so long ago.

II

The first question asked of Jesus had to do with this matter of the source of his authority. It is so easy when we hear a new idea to ask, "Who says so?" Actually, the only significant question is, "Is it true?" Jesus was a very clever speaker, and could handle questions very well. It's not just a Yankee trait to answer a question with another question, for this was the rabbinic method long before there were any "Yankees." When Jesus was asked by whose authority he did the things he did, he posed another question in answer: "Whence came the baptism of John?" Thus his questioners were impaled on the horns of a dilemma. They couldn't answer his question; he refused to answer theirs in the way they asked it. He continued and gave the story of the vineyard. This is a hard parable, overcast with notes of tragedy and destruction; but the light shines through if we recognize that the destruction in the world that follows upon the rejection of God's purpose is not because God is vengeful, but because of the nature of the universe.

The fall and destruction of earlier civilizations is not the action of a vengeful, capricious God. Gibbons and other historians see the dissolution of the Roman Empire and the fall of other civilizations as the result of disease that grew within them from the rejection of fundamental moral principles. "The very stone which the builders rejected has become the head of the corner. Every one who falls on that stone will be broken to pieces; but when it falls on any one it will crush him," said Jesus, quoting a psalm (Luke 20:17). In the physical realm, the law of gravity is not going to be changed just because I happen to dislike it, nor are the laws of health going to be changed just because I happen to dislike them. I have the choice either of abiding by the law of gravity and the rules of health or of being destroyed. It is not a vengeful God who will destroy me, or the laws either. I will be destroying myself. The person who humorously says, "Everything I like is either illegal, immoral, or fattening," is not making a very significant comment about the universe but is saying something very important about himself.

Jesus said in another context, "By their fruits ye shall know them" (Matt. 7:20, K.J.V.). The test, the result, the fruit is the final indication of worth. Is he not saying that truth is self-authenticating? Truth does not gain its status because a lot of prominent people have supported it. People become prominent because they have adopted and followed the truth. Truth does not depend upon personal prestige. By whose authority? No, is it true? Truth is self-authenticating, when it is examined from all sides. In the clash of opinion, truth emerges.

The second question raised in this context was the question of temporal loyalty. Those who posed the question hoped to trap Jesus. Either he would appear unpatriotic to the Jews or disloyal to the Romans. This was a ticklish situation—almost like the classic unanswerable question, "Have you left off beating your wife yet?" Some questions cannot be answered with a simple yes or no.

"Is it lawful for us to give tribute to Caesar, or not?" No one likes to pay taxes, but in Jesus' day the paying of taxes was a symbol of the exploitation and degradation of the people, a captive nation. Where does your loyalty lie? With your country or with God? This implies a conflict between the two with one forced to choose between loyalty to country and loyalty to God. Jesus said, "Show me a coin." After commenting on the inscription and superscription, he made the statement, "Render to Caesar the things that are Caesar's, and to God the things that are God's." They could not trap him.

This verse is often quoted to justify rendering to country without any thought of God, or vice versa. Jesus mentioned both. A person should be loyal to his community, to his state, to his country, but his loyalty to these can only be expressed adequately if he has a higher loyalty to God. There is no conflict between loyalty to God and loyalty to country. They are on different planes. True loyalty to country is not expressed by unquestioning and uncritical acquiescence to all its temporal demands. Where it seems the action of the country is contrary to the will of God, the person who surrenders his right of critical judgment is not really serving his nation either, any more than the parent who finds that the desires of his child run counter to the child's best interest is really helping the child by giving in to his whim and, perhaps, permitting death or serious injury. Of course the Christian is loyal to his nation, but he does not express that loyalty by surrendering his critical judgment, for this is neither loving country nor serving God. Richard Lovelace, the sentimental poet of the seventeenth century, expressed a profound truth when he wrote upon leaving for military service,

> I could not love thee, dear, so much,
> Loved I not Honour more.[2]

We cannot love country truly unless we love God more—unless we see that our obligation to our country, to our community, to all our social relations, is constantly to work for their improvement in line with God's purpose.

Now consider the last point emphasized during this day of creative controversy. Jesus was sitting on that side of the courtyard where the offering boxes were placed. He was watching people go by —all kinds of people. There were those who, at no cost to themselves, maybe even out of a tax advantage, were putting their offerings into the box. Then a woman came by. One can almost see the amazed joy with which Jesus noted the commitment of this widow. Do not make the mistake of assuming that Jesus is suggesting some impossible practice of requiring that everyone should impoverish himself and give away his whole living. This is not the point. The point being made is that conscientious commitment costs. Giving from the overflow, giving that costs nothing doesn't mean much. The programs that are supported in this way can make

[2] "To Lucasta, on Going to the Wars."

good use of the receipts. But giving is not just for the sake of supporting activities. We give because we need to be identified with worth-while activity. Giving, whether of substance, time, or talents, that costs nothing is far below the most meaningful experience for the giver.

One of the great Lenten hymns is "Beneath the Cross of Jesus, I Fain Would Take My Stand." Elizabeth Clephane did not write the words to this hymn in a vacuum or merely to have some nice words to sing during Lent. She was a woman who devoted herself to the service of others in emulation of her Lord. On one occasion she sold her carriage and her horses in order that she might have more substance to serve the needy. Had it not been for this willingness, this commitment, this dedication, she could not have had the spiritual experience that made it possible for her to express the profound religious emotion and truth found in that hymn.

III

There are many lessons we might learn from this day of creative controversy in the life of our Lord. Controversy there will always be. We hope it may be creative controversy, but creative controversy will always lead to conscientious commitment. Three points were made by Jesus: First, truth is self-authenticating. One cannot prove love in the laboratory but one cannot deny the love of man for wife, of parent for child. One cannot ignore Jesus Christ, Francis of Assisi, Albert Schweitzer, to name but three.

Second, loyalty to less than the highest is a betrayal of the lesser loyalty as well. True patriotism is a desire to make one's country the best possible instrument of God's purpose.

Third, commitment without cost has little meaning. In the words of the knight who heard them as he shared his crust of bread with a beggar beside the road:

> Not what we give, but what we share,
> For the gift without the giver is bare;
> Who gives himself with his alms feeds three,
> Himself, his hungering neighbor, and Me.[3]

Thanks be to God for the wondrous gift of grace in Christ Jesus, and the sure knowledge of his continuing concern, for truly, the stone which the builders rejected has become the head of the corner.

---

[3] James Russell Lowell, *The Vision of Sir Launfal*, II, 8.

WEDNESDAY

The Day of Retirement and Relaxation

Scripture Lesson:
Mark 14:3-11 (cf. Luke 7:36-50)

As a boy i can remember spending many Sunday afternoons looking at a scroll of religious pictures that had belonged to my father. This scroll, which was put together long before the days of improved methods of audio-visual education, consisted of a set of small pictures illustrating the events of the Old Testament and a larger set of pictures (reproductions of great paintings for the most part) illustrating the life of Jesus. By turning a small crank, the pictures would pass before one's eyes.

One of the pictures from the life of Jesus has stuck in my memory. It shows Jesus sitting on what was the equivalent of a porch, overlooking the valley. Presumably he is in Judea. He is surrounded by a group of friends and is conversing with them in a very relaxed way as they look out over the valley. Most of the representations of Jesus that we see portray him in the midst of action or show him in some symbolic experience. This picture, however, showed him simply relaxing with friends.

There is something very appealing and attractive about the picture. As we consider the events of the last week as recorded by Luke and try to put these events into the framework of a week, a curious fact emerges: One day is missing. The day corresponding to the first Sunday was the day of the triumphal entry. On the day corresponding to Monday, there was the cleansing of the Temple. On the day corresponding to Tuesday, there was the discussion in the Temple courtyard. On Thursday there was the institution of the Last Supper; Friday was the day of the trial and the Crucifixion; Saturday was the day of sorrow and silence and the first day of the week (Sunday again) was the day of resurrection. In Luke's account there is no record of anything happening on Wednesday.

The other two Synoptics do record, "two days before the Passover," one event which deals with an incident at the home of Simon the leper in Bethany. It is very similar to Luke's account of "a woman of the city, who was a sinner" (7:37), which has been placed at another point in the narrative. For our purposes, we shall restore this incident to the Holy Week setting. Because, however, Luke's account is somewhat confused and set in a different context, we shall turn to the version in Mark.

One can speculate that Jesus spent the day in question as a day of relaxed retirement with friends, following upon three very stirring and exhausting days and prior to two very difficult, climactic days. There is something very appealing about the figure of Jesus relaxing with his friends in the midst of this greatest of weeks and then going later to a "dinner party" with other friends.

I

Recall to mind what must have been the scene in Bethany during the last week. Thousands of persons had come to Jerusalem for the Passover, as was the custom. The accounts in the Scriptures indicate that there was not room for Jesus in the city, for in each case it tells how he came in in the morning. It has been assumed that he spent the time with Mary, Martha, Lazarus, and perhaps some others, in Bethany. Jesus relaxed here, gathering his energies. He was accustomed to going out by himself for solitary prayer; and because of this, it is easy to overlook the number of instances in the New Testament where Jesus had what was little more than just an evening of friendly fellowship with acquaintances. He was criticized by John the Baptist and his disciples for going to banquets and "dinner parties." Those who feel that this kind of activity is out of character for the religious person overlook the fact that Jesus himself found joy in the companionship of other people. Solitary prayer, of course. But also friendly fellowship with others.

The person who feels that in order to be religious one must drive, drive, drive; that one must always have a long face; that there is never an opportunity for a smile or a laugh, does not know Jesus. There are many flashes of humor in the words of Jesus. The oriental hyperbole which he used so often contains the light, and often merry, touch. There is relaxed companionship with other people in Jesus. Never, of course, did he lose sight of his fundamental purpose, but he recognized the rhythm that there is in life—the need to go away and recoup one's energies for the next forward plunge. When the tide comes in, it does not come up evenly. The waves rush in and then recede a bit; then up and back. Gradually, however, as the tide comes in, the waterline comes farther and farther up the shore. So it is in life. There are times for driving; there are times for relaxation. The streams that turn the wheels of industry take their rise in quiet places.

It is never, however, either/or; it is always both/and. Do not go out and say, "Well, all you have to do to be religious is to put your feet up and relax! The preacher said so." This is hardly the point. But neither is it the point to say that all you need to do to be religious is drive, drive, drive. In this way you may end up with a case of ulcers, but

52

not necessarily any closer to the kingdom of God! There is alternation in life between activity and rest. There is a place for casual companionship; there is a place for relaxed friendliness; there is a place for joy.

There is joy in Jesus and there is joy in the true Christian. This is the joy that proceeds from an appreciation of other people. Will Rogers is supposed to have said: "I never met a man I didn't like!" One might react to this by saying, "What's wrong with Will Rogers? He must be crazy. All the people he met—there must have been somebody he didn't like!" His statement, "I never met a man I didn't like," is not a comment on the people he had met so much as it is a profound comment on himself —the kind of person he was.

Note these words of Thomas Merton, the contemplative monk: "Hell is where no one has anything in common with anybody else except the fact that they all hate one another, and cannot get away from one another and from themselves." [1] Hell is not an imaginary place of punishment after the experience of physical death; hell is any place where no one shares anything in common with anyone else except the fact that they hate one another and can escape neither from one another nor from themselves.

In direct contrast to this somber background

[1] *Seeds of Contemplation* (New York: New Directions, 1949), p. 60.

notice the light of the wonder and glory of Jesus in relaxed companionship with his friends. There is a place for this kind of fellowship.

II

In the Gospel according to Mark is the beautiful account of the spontaneous outpouring of devotion which brought shocked remonstrance from the beholders and perceptive appreciation from Jesus. Jesus was dining at the home of Simon in Bethany when an unnamed woman came in with an alabaster jar of pure, costly ointment, broke it, and anointed Jesus' head with it. Had you been there, what would your reaction have been? In Luke's similar story, the woman is called "a sinner" and the story, in a different setting, is used as an entrance into a discussion about forgiveness. Mark's and Matthew's accounts do not identify the woman at all. There is no need to speculate upon the cause for her adoration of Jesus. Simply see it for what it was—an unselfish act of complete devotion. The value of her gift may set the perspective. One commentator computes the value at $240,[2] while another places it at about $500 [3] in our money. What a waste! But wait a moment.

[2] Frederick C. Grant in *The Interpreter's Bible* (Nashville: Abingdon Press, 1951), "Exegesis," VII, 868.

[3] *Mission and Message of Jesus: An exposition of the Gospels in the light of modern research* (New York: E. P. Dutton & Co., Inc., 1938), p. 165.

Some years ago a church group of high-school young people was on a tour of one of our large cities. They were visiting some of the great churches located there. While walking down the side aisle of one of the largest and most ornate of the churches the group stopped briefly in front of the various side altars to examine the memorial inscriptions and to consider the symbolism and beauty of each one. One young man in the party became increasingly agitated as the tour continued. Finally he could contain himself no more, and he burst out: "I think this is sinful! Think of all the money that's been poured into this stuff that could have been used to help the poor and to clear some of those awful slums we've seen! I think this is terrible!" Did not his comment reflect the same feeling as that of the men in Bethany who indignantly objected because the ointment was not sold and the money given to the poor?

We should not infer from this that we need not be concerned about the poor and needy and that instead, we should put all our substance into expensive gestures. No. Jesus, by saying, "You always have the poor with you," was *not* implying that we should ignore our obligation to them. Far from it. In fact, he flatly states, "Whenever you will, you *can* do good to them." Rather those who often think of the religious life merely as a process of doing good, need to recognize the need for spontaneous adoration. Those who sometimes think in cold, stark terms need to recall the importance of beauty. Here again, it is not a case of either/or but both/and. Love of neighbor, of course. But also the ecstasy of adoration. The comment of Jesus is unforgettable: "She has done a beautiful thing." As he said, this can never be forgotten.

Or consider this from a slightly different angle. Many clergymen are concerned about the fees which come to them, particularly funeral fees. Some flatly refuse them, or automatically return them. An older and wiser pastor and I were discussing this one day, and he told me of an incident which occurred in the early years of his ministry. He had had a funeral for a man in his church who, in the opinion of this pastor, was not very well off. When he received a check from the widow in appreciation of his service, he returned it to her. Later, in conversation with him, she dropped the phrase: "Since you refused my attempt to say 'Thank you.'" Do we, thoughtlessly, though from the finest of motives, sometimes prevent people from expressing gratitude? How easily the words leap to our lips, "Oh, you shouldn't have done it!" Contrast the gracious acceptance by Jesus of an act of spontaneous devotion.

The late Halford E. Luccock expressed it like this:

There is permanent meaning here which is never exhausted. The question comes up again and again, usually with a sour note from the shortsighted, "Why spend money on churches when there are hungry people in the world?" The answer is not only that true worship is life's inherently greatest experience, and needs no justification in dollars and cents, but also that it is an unfailing fountainhead of generous service. Devotion to God is a well, springing up eternally, out of which flow great streams for the healing and blessing of men. The devotion represented by the breaking of the alabaster box, the outgoing of affection and honor for Christ, has been the source of the greatest help to the poor the world has ever known. It works out in a paradox: If we see life only in terms of denarii which ought to be better distributed, and grow blind to the intangibles—like "Thou shalt love the Lord thy God with all thy heart"—soon there will not be very many denarii to distribute." [4]

Service and worship, worship and service—both are essential.

III

Following the relaxation with friends and the gracious acceptance of an act of homage comes the beginning of betrayal. Who can finally say what motivated Judas? Was it he who spoke the words of condemnation of the act of adoration of the woman referred to earlier? After all, it was Judas who acted as treasurer for the band of disciples. Did this final act of impractical idealism on the part of Jesus finally convince Judas that Jesus would never

[4] Halford E. Luccock in *The Interpreter's Bible, op. cit.*, "Exposition," p. 870.

make a good leader for his nation? Could it be that Jesus was not turning out to be the kind of Messiah Judas wanted him to be, and so he refused to let Jesus make him the kind of disciple needed? Do these questions and observations stab each of us?

This much is certain: whatever Judas first found to lead him to follow Jesus had been displaced in his soul by some other loyalty. His tragic figure stands as a somber reminder of the ease with which the highest loyalty can be displaced by a lesser loyalty.

IV

Quiet relaxation, the gracious acceptance of a spontaneous gift of love against the gathering darkness of betrayal and suffering—these mark the day in the middle of history's greatest week. Two poets sound these notes.

William Wordsworth's familiar lines reflect our own experience:

> The world is too much with us; late and soon,
> Getting and spending, we lay waste our powers.[5]

Let us beware lest we reverse the thought as if anything that is not getting and spending were the waste!

John Greenleaf Whittier did not consider himself a hymn writer. Yet some favorite hymns have

[5] "The World Is Too Much with Us."

come from his poems. His long seventeen-stanza poem, "The Brewing of Soma" tells of the making of an intoxicating drink by members of a certain sect in India. After describing the process he calls to the reader's attention certain equally pagan practices in his own [and our own] day. He then extols the restfulness of the higher life with the words:

> Dear Lord and Father of mankind!
>   Forgive our feverish ways!
> Reclothe us in our rightful mind,
> In purer lives Thy service find,
>   In deeper reverence, praise.

As Jesus faced the horrible experiences of the rest of the week, one cannot but marvel at the fact that he was the quietest, the calmest, and the most self-possessed person there.

There is a place for activity in life. There is also place for quiet relaxation.

MAUNDY
THURSDAY

The Day of Intimate Fellowship

Scripture Lesson: Luke 22:7-30, 39-46

IN THE FACE OF GREAT DECISION AND GREAT CHAL-
lenge, where do you turn for assistance? Whence
come strength and sustaining power? Do they not
come from intimate fellowship?

We have seen Jesus as he moved through the
great events of his last week. He is now approaching
the crisis. He has heard the plaudits of the crowd.
He has reacted on an emotional level to conditions
he found in the city. He has engaged in spirited
and creative—but also exhausting—controversy.
He has withdrawn for refreshment in the relaxed
company of friends. Now refreshed, he moves on to
the next part of the great drama of redemption. He
is entering into the experience of intimate fellow-

ship which will supply strength necessary for the agony to come.

This intimate fellowship was—and is—experienced on two planes. The symbol of the cross calls to mind many things. With its horizontal and vertical arms, it illustrates that at the center of human experience are found both a horizontal and a vertical relationship. In the life of Jesus, these are supremely illustrated in the Upper Room and in the Garden of Gethsemane.

I

After the relaxation in Bethany, Jesus moved into the intimate fellowship of those who had struggled with him; who had endured with him; who had gone through trials with him—the fellowship of dedicated discipleship.

As we read the description of the location of the Upper Room, we could assume that here again is an example of the clairvoyance of Jesus, a kind of semimiracle. He saw, as in a vision, a man carrying a pitcher of water, and told the disciples to follow him to where they would find the Upper Room. It may be, however, that this was a prearranged signal; that the family in whose home the Upper Room was located was a part of the larger Christian fellowship. There has been speculation on the basis of information in Acts as well as from other sources, that the Upper Room may have been located in the house of the parents of young John Mark, who wrote the oldest of the Gospel accounts. The mother of John Mark was a member of the early Christian community. At any rate, there was an upper room in which Jesus and the Twelve could gather together to prepare and eat the Passover meal.

A Jewish scholar could point out that apparently the writer of Luke was not fully aware of all the ritualistic details in the Passover meal. This, however, is not important. The important thing is that here Jesus was having a farewell meal with his intimate companions and was also establishing a symbolic act to bolster, inspire, and direct them down through the unknown days to come. It is interesting to note that, in Luke's account, unlike the usual ritual, Jesus offered the cup first and then the bread.

Note that the supper did not *create* fellowship; rather, it was an event which *recognized* and *celebrated* the fellowship of the believers and those who had worked intimately together. This was not an occasion to which all were invited and urged to come. Does not the Sacrament of the Lord's Supper celebrate, rather then create, a fellowship which is both horizontal and vertical? At any rate, this was an intimate fellowship of dedicated discipleship.

Note the statement made about the anticipated betrayal. In Luke's account, the betrayer is not specifically identified. There is only the general statement that "the hand of him who betrays me is with me on the table." Presumably, all of them had their hands on the table. Note their puzzlement: "Is it I, Lord?" They began to question one another —*Am I the one?* Each of us faces that question. In one sense the Twelve began to betray him immediately, for they began to argue about who was the greatest; who was the most important; who would have the pre-eminent place in the new kingdom. This led to Jesus' statement about the nature of greatness—a statement applicable not only in the time of the Apostles, but today as well. It was Napoleon in exile who said, "Alexander and I founded our empires on force. Jesus alone founded his on love, and to this day, countless thousands would die for him." There follows that supreme humbling expression, as Jesus says, "But I am among you as one who serves."

One of the supreme experiences of fellowship is the fellowship of service. In the summer of 1955, in the course of twenty-four hours, fourteen inches of rain were dumped on western Connecticut. In this area is the town of Winsted. Through this town there runs a small stream, which is usually little more than a trickle. This peaceful little brook is called the Mad River—which always seemed the strangest of names until that August day in 1955 when the fourteen-inch rainfall funneled down through that river along with water from an overflowing lake up in the hills, and the little brook in the valley was transformed into a raging, destructive torrent. The Mad River lived up to its name! All the buildings along its shore in Winsted were either demolished outright or severely damaged; the main street of the town was washed away.

John Hersey, Pulitzer-prize author, wrote a piece for the *New Yorker* magazine describing the experience of the people in Winsted. He told of the work of rescue and the impromptu emergency service carried on in the midst of this tragic event. He talked about the camaraderie of those who had been bound together in this experience of serving in the rescue work. He talked about people who had lived all their lives in this community and had nodded to one another on the street, perhaps, but never really had known one another. Suddenly they found themselves together in the same rowboat taking some people from a condemned building or pulling on the same rope by which others were drawn to safety. There was born a camaraderie, a companionship, a fellowship of service and suffering that bound those people together. How tragic that so often this type of togetherness can come only from trouble and catastrophe!

In the J. Arthur Rank production of *Albert Schweitzer* there is presented an unforgettable picture of the life and work of this modern saint. In the movie, Dr. Schweitzer uses a phrase about the fellowship of pain—the fellowship of those who have suffered pain. He goes on to talk about the fellowship and obligation of those who have been rescued from pain to do something for those who still must suffer.

Two days after the Russian satellite began to whirl around the earth, there appeared in the *New York Times* this statement:

The creature who descended from a tree or crawled out of a cave a few thousand years ago is now on the eve of incredible journeys. Yet it is not these journeys which chiefly matter. Will we be happier for seeing the other side of the moon or strolling among the Martian meadows? . . . The greatest adventure of all is not to go to the moon or explore the rings of Saturn. It is rather, to understand the heart and soul of man and to turn away from wrath and destruction and toward creativeness and brotherly love.[1]

Jesus said, "I am among you as one who serves." Casual companionship and friendly fellowship have their place. The Christian must move on to dedicated discipleship and the fellowship of serving.

II

Beyond the horizontal fellowship, no matter how intimate, there is another type. After Jesus and the others had sung a hymn, they went out into a garden on the Mount of Olives called Gethsemane. Mark the name—"Gethsemane"—the place of the olive press. Here the fruit was taken and subjected

[1] Editorial in *The New York Times,* October 7, 1957, p. 26. Used by permission.

to tremendous pressure in order that the essence might be drawn forth—the olive oil. Here, too, Jesus was subjected to tremendous pressure that the essence might be and was drawn forth. We, too, have our Gethsemanes.

There in Gethsemane, Jesus experienced his third great temptation. There are three great temptations in the life of Jesus. The first, after his baptism, was to use his gifts and talents for less than the highest good. The second, on the mountain called the "Mount of Transfiguration," was to "play it safe"; to stay up in Galilee away from Jerusalem and the danger awaiting there. The third temptation, in Gethsemane, was to run away—to escape. "Let this cup pass from me." Let me escape my task and duty.

> His heart craved sympathy,
>   But He was alone.
> He was fighting the battle for all the race,
>   And He was alone.
> He was pitted against all the powers of hell,
>   And He was alone.
> He was lonely—desperately lonely,
>   And He was alone! [2]

There is a terrible loneliness about great decisions. A well-known painting depicts a Colonial

[2] From *Christ and the Fine Arts* by Cynthia Maus (rev. ed.; New York: Harper & Brothers, 1959). Reprinted by special permission of the author-compiler.

general kneeling in the snow at Valley Forge—
alone. It is not irreverent to note a certain similarity
between this picture and paintings of Jesus in the
garden. Or take a picture of a man in 1861 and
compare it with a picture of that same man in 1865.
Notice the lines etched upon his face. Abraham
Lincoln looked not four years older but four times
four years older. The 1865 painting reflected those
long nights of which he spoke, when, in the quiet
city of Washington, footsteps echoed along the
upper corridor of the White House as this man
faced terrible decisions—*alone.* Regardless of po-
litical affiliation, when one looks at a picture of
Franklin Roosevelt taken in 1941 and compares it
with a picture of him taken in 1945, the aging
process is apparent. Here was a man who, although
he could not stride the upper corridors of the White
House, spent sleepless nights struggling with the
great decisions—*alone.* Harry Truman testified that
the biggest single burden of the presidency—as it is
for all persons in positions of great authority—is
that after all the opinions are in, all the data
gathered, and all discussion completed, the decision
must be made—*alone.*

This is not confined to leaders of men. Every one
of us is faced with the necessity of making decisions
—*alone.* In a great crisis, each person is alone. Many
have had the experience of lying on a stretcher outside the operating room, grateful for the concern of
others, thankful for the skill of those who shall min-

ister to physical needs, but yet, in a very real sense, *alone*. Everyone has spent hours at night struggling with the question, "How shall I answer that letter?" "What shall I say tomorrow?" "How shall I decide this question?" We can ask for advice; we can search for understanding; we can share the problems; but we make the decisions *alone*.

There comes a time when human fellowship can no longer assist, when the edge of human fellowship is reached. Then, supremely miserable is he who has none other to fall back upon! Jesus could, out of his human longing, say to the disciples, "Could ye not watch with me one hour?" (K.J.V.). It is easy to be hard on the disciples. But in a very profound sense, the answer to the question must be "No!" Not that they could not have avoided falling asleep, but it was impossible for them to enter into the depths of their Master's experience. This he had to face *alone*.

But in a far more important way, he was not alone! Nor need we be! If religion is what a man does with his solitude, then here in the garden is the supreme example of what religion was for Jesus, has been for many, and can be for all. When one reaches the edge of the bolstering of human companionship and human fellowship—the horizontal fellowship—there is waiting the vertical fellowship of him who is always our Shepherd; who accompanies us "into the woods" where the Master went, and even unto the end of the world, in a vital, sustaining relationship. The key to the experience is the phrase, "Nevertheless not my will, but thine, be done."

The experience of Jesus in Gethsemane is sometimes used to prove that God does not answer prayer. If ever there was a righteous request, the petition of Jesus was it. Yet, it was refused—or so it seems. But wait a moment. Something far more important was granted. There came with the submission to the will of God, the strength necessary to the task ahead. There came a sense of significance and the sustaining presence of God the Father.

III

There are two kinds of fellowship in this day in the life of Jesus: the intimate fellowship of those bound together by common service and the sustaining fellowship, in great trouble and need, of his heavenly Father. Each of us may experience both.

However,

When he prays, a man must risk growing more like Jesus of Nazareth; and being like Jesus of Nazareth in a world like this is not a prospect to be viewed with composure. To love where love is crucified; to be unselfish where the crowd will take advantage of your unselfishness, cheat you for being honest, and hurt your feelings for showing yourself affectionate! It may be that God will answer your prayer as you stand naked and alone before him: risking what you are on what he is! [3]

[3] Paul Scherer in *The Interpreter's Bible* (Nashville: Abingdon Press, 1952) , "Exposition," VIII, 390.

And you will be conscious of the fact that true blessedness is not mostly pleasure, but mostly victory—victory through the strength that comes from submission to God the Father.

Thanks be to him for the assurance, "Lo, I am with you alway, even unto the end of the world" (K.J.V.).

GOOD FRIDAY

The Day of Suffering

Scripture Lesson:
Selections from Luke 22 and 23

Were you there when they crucified my Lord?

. . . .

Were you there when they nailed Him to the tree?

. . . .

Were you there when they pierced Him in the side?

. . . .

Were you there when the sun refused to shine?

. . . .

Were you there when they laid Him in the tomb?

. . . .

Were you there when they crucified my Lord?

PERHAPS YOU'VE SUNG THOSE WORDS TO A PLAINTIVE
tune; perhaps you've heard others sing this Negro
spiritual. Perhaps you remember the words

71

Sometimes it causes me to tremble, tremble;
Were you there when they crucified my Lord?

Of course the answer is "No" in the flesh, but at least once a year (and perhaps it would be good if it were more often than once a year), we try to be there in understanding, in spiritual experience. Here is both the central mystery and the central meaning of life as the Christian sees it. We have the advantage of hindsight and know that this is not the whole story, but we can never understand the meaning of Easter apart from the tragic, horrible experience of Good Friday.

Bishop James H. Straughn suggested that we reverse our perspective on the cross. Instead of always looking up at it from below, we should try, in imagination and without irreverence, to transpose ourselves and see what Jesus saw from the cross: his loved ones close by; the soldiers, forced to carry out an unpleasant duty, relieving the tension a bit by gambling for his robe; those who were supposed to be the leaders of their people but whose blindness and self-concern had led them to mock and reject Him; the large crowds in the city, composed of ordinary people, most of whom were oblivious to what was happening just outside the city gates. Beyond, we would see the Temple with its mystery and its many practices which served to separate the people from God rather than to reveal him to them. Is not this the meaning of the rending of the veil of the Temple from the top to the bottom? Does not this say that on Calvary all that might hide the depths of God's love for man was torn away? The veil referred to is that before the Holy of Holies in the Temple through which even the high priest entered but once a year. Here on Calvary is the Holy of Holies of sacrificial love completely revealed. Beyond the Temple is the horizon and beyond the horizon, the infinite. All are included in the crucifixion scene.

Following the days of temporary triumph, emotion, creative controversy, retirement, fellowship, we approach the climax; yet at the same time, we also shrink from it. We would avoid suffering. Yet only through suffering can we understand life. We are, here, face to face with the ultimate. In Luke's account, there are two dominant themes running through the events. On the one hand there are those who wish to avoid responsibility—to evade the problem posed by Jesus, to be done with it as easily as possible. On the other hand there is the acceptance by Jesus of the worst that man can do, assured that God cannot be defeated and that his purpose of good can only be postponed, but not destroyed. Avoidance and evasion, acceptance and assurance. So walk in imagination the path of this day of suffering.

I

Note first the travesty of the trials, as indications of the desire to avoid responsibility. Jesus was turning the world upside down with his preaching of the brotherhood of all men. His attack upon privilege in high places, his concern that all men might be saved caused him to be seized by the leaders of his own people. They wished to get him out of the way before he could damage their positions. Being a captive people, they did not have the right to put anyone to death. At their council meeting they could only work out a scheme by which sentence of death would be pronounced by the Roman governor. The high priest asked cynically, *Is it not better that one man be done away with than that the nation be turned upside down?* (This is, of course, a paraphrase of one of the other accounts.) How do we answer that question when it refers to someone in our own day who raises uncomfortable questions about our social order?

Following the appearance before the high priest, Jesus was taken to Pilate. The Roman procurator had apparently attained his high position by a fortuitous marriage as well as by a certain bulldog capacity in the military arts. He was crafty in maintaining his position. He did not want to condemn this man, but he could not destroy his rapport with the Jewish leaders. Then a way out appeared. Learning that Jesus was originally from Galilee, he hurried him off to Herod who was in Jerusalem for the Passover.

Herod apparently anticipated entertaining his friends with Jesus! We read: "When Herod saw

Jesus, he was delighted, for he had been wanting to see him for a long time. He had heard a lot about Jesus and was hoping to see him perform a miracle." (Luke 23:8, Phillips.) When no satisfaction was obtained, he contemptuously arrayed Jesus in a purple robe, mocking him, and sent him back to Pilate. After all, he had no grounds for condemnation either. We see the cynicism of the high priest, the craftiness of Pilate, and the contemptuous treatment of Herod. There follows an attempt at compromise by Pilate.

Still anxious to escape responsibility, Pilate said: *I'll chastize him. I'll have him scourged and then turn him loose, because there's really nothing wrong here.* Three times he tried, but each time he was unable to find an acceptable compromise. When basic principle is involved, can one ever compromise without destroying everything? Ah, yes, the give-and-take that involves a reconciliation of different points of view is always worthy, but where basic principle is involved, no compromise is possible. So, surrendering to the group, Pilate turned Jesus over to be scourged—whipped with a "cat-o'-nine-tails" into which were braided bits of metal so that the quivering flesh of the back was ripped raw and bleeding.

II

Following the trials, Jesus was turned over to be tortured at the hands of the soldiers. Their unthinking brutality proceeded partly from their desire to escape from their own responsibility. Often the greatest cruelty proceeds not from the basic nature of a man, but from the man's insecurity and uncertainty in the face of a problem with which he cannot quite cope. We need look no farther than some of the statements of Nazi concentration camp commanders for twentieth-century illustrations of this fact.

After the horrible scourging came the way of tears through the city. It is regrettable that there is nothing in Protestantism that corresponds to the emotional involvement of the Roman Catholic as he makes the Stations of the Cross. To be sure, this type of ritualistic observance cannot be meaningful for us, but our tendency to ignore this aspect of suffering is not good, either.

Then came the nailing to the cross. Cecil DeMille has done some things to the Bible in his films that are pretty bad. However, many years ago he produced a silent film entitled *King of Kings*. It was not of uniform excellence, but one scene packed a terrific wallop. Although made before the advent of sound motion pictures, it continued to be shown for many years with sound dubbed into the background. In the crucifixion scene the hammering of the nails was off camera. When the sound was dubbed into the film, most of it consisted of mood music, as one would expect. At the crucifixion scene, however, all music stopped and the only sound in the theater or auditorium where the picture was being shown was the dull thud of a mallet striking upon a nail. So great is the power of suggestion that those who saw and heard could almost feel the thud of nails against their own flesh.

III

After the travesty of the trials and the brutal physical torture came the Crucifixion itself.

One of the most interesting things about the Gospel accounts of the Passion are the statements from the cross that are recalled by the individual writers. The writer of Matthew relates one; the writer of Mark, the same one. The writer of John includes three different statements, and Luke has three which appear nowhere else. In each case these statements reflect the purpose of each writer running through his whole Gospel account. Consider the three given by Luke:

The first one is the statement of forgiveness, "Father, forgive them; for they know not what they do." We are reminded of the humble American GI on Luzon who lost his life in the action there. After his death, his parents found in his papers explicit instructions that, if anything should happen to him, he wanted his GI insurance used to establish a scholarship in order that after the war a Japanese boy might study at one of our universities. "Father, forgive, them; for they know not what they do."

The taunt of the crowd, "He saved others; himself he cannot save" (K.J.V.) , completely missed the point that he *could* have. He might have run away! The crowd missed completely the fact that there are situations in which, in order to save others, one cannot save oneself. The young man who leaps into the boiling torrent and saves a child that has been swept away but who, in the process, hits his head upon a stone in the rapids and loses his own life illustrates this truth. How infinitely great the love of One whose free giving of himself is revealed supremely on Calvary against the knowledge that he could have escaped! The taunt of the crowd is actually a tribute and might be paraphrased, "He saved others because he refused to save himself!"

The second statement recalled by Luke is the statement of concern for the thief. We know not how to describe in any literal sense the promise that is made, but note the wonder of Jesus' concern for others in the midst of his own physical agony. Three were crucified on Golgotha, that skull-shaped hill in the middle of the city dump. Two were crucified because they were so bad—so far below the normal level of goodness. One was crucified because he was so far above the general level of goodness. We react with wonder to his concern for the penitent thief: "Today shalt thou be with me in paradise" (K.J.V.) .

The last statement, "Father, into thy hands I commend my spirit!" is less a statement of resignation than a description of the state of all his life. This is a state to which we all may aspire. "Nothing can separate us from the love of God, which is in Christ Jesus our Lord." (Rom. 8:39, K.J.V., *paraphrased.*)

IV

Before the cross there can be nothing but awe-struck gratitude. There come to mind the words of the prophet in Lamentations: "Is it nothing to you, all ye that pass by? behold, and see if there be any sorrow like unto my sorrow, which is done unto me, wherewith the Lord hath afflicted me in the day of his fierce anger" (1:12, K.J.V.). For

From the Throne of His Cross, the King of grief
Cries out to a world of unbelief:
Oh! men and women, afar and nigh,
Is it nothing to you, all ye that pass by?

I laid my eternal power aside,
I came from the home of the glorified,
A babe, in the lowly cave to lie;
Is it nothing to you, all ye that pass by?

.   .   .   .

Behold me and see: piercèd through and through
With countless sorrows—and all is for you;
For you I suffer, for you I die;
Is it nothing to you, all ye that pass by?

Oh! men and women, your deeds of shame,
Your sins without reason and number and name,
I bear them all on this Cross on high;
Is it nothing to you, all ye that pass by?

.   .   .   .

Oh come unto me! by the woes I have borne,
By the dreadful scourge, and the crown of thorn,
By these I implore you to hear my cry;
Is it nothing to you, all ye that pass by?

Oh come unto me! this awful price,
Redemption's tremendous sacrifice,
Is paid for you.—Oh, why will ye die?
Is it nothing to you, all ye that pass by? [1]

Thanks be to God it *is* something to us who pass by. The Christian church is that fellowship of persons who, looking at the cross, know that it was for them; that there is a fellowship which binds them to him; and that great and glorious is the privilege of ministering in his spirit and in his name.

Yes, it *is* something to us. It is *all* to us.

[1] "The Appeal of the Crucified." From *The Crucifixion* by John Stainer. Used by permission of G. Schirmer, Inc.

EASTER DAY

The Day of Eternal Triumph

Scripture Lesson: **Luke 23:50–24:11, 36-53**

"He is risen!"

"He is risen, indeed!"

HOW MANY MILLIONS OF THROATS HAVE ECHOED that glad cry and response down through the ages of the Christian Era! This exultant statement and its reply became a password in the early church. One Christian would greet another on Easter morning with the proclamation, "He is risen!" to which the countersign was, "He is risen, indeed!" This separated the Christians from the pagans—those who were of the fellowship and those who were not. It still does, though the words are not used in the same way!

Note particularly the tense of the verb. Not "he has risen," but "he is risen." This is not the memory of a long-past event, but the proclamation of a continuing state of being—not a finished thing, but a continuing experience. It is in this spirit that Easter must be celebrated now—not as an isolated observance, but as an integral part of life.

Contrast the celebration of Easter in our day, with millions participating, with the first Easter. It comes as a bit of a surprise and a shock to us to note how little effect the first Easter had on the city of Jerusalem. There were no throngs flocking to the empty tomb; there were no crowds gathering to sing praises. Indeed, very few persons knew anything about the Resurrection on that first Easter. Palm Sunday may represent only the day of temporary triumph, but the event was noticed in the city. Crowds flocked to Jesus on that day—even though they quickly fell away. Had there been a daily newspaper in Jerusalem, however, it is doubtful if any notice at all of the great event of resurrection would have appeared in it on the Monday after. Only those few who had previously known Jesus intimately were raised from despair into hope; from the depths to the heights. Indeed, there was less notice of his resurrection, according to the Gospel accounts, than there was of his birth, humble though that was. His birth was announced to three Magi and to certain anonymous shepherds who shared it with others of the town. Not so with the Resurrection.

Easter is the day of eternal triumph. There is a difference between the temporary hailing of something and the eternal acceptance of it. Perhaps therein lies the key to our dilemma. On this joyous day, the happiest of the year, it may be pointed out that: the first Easter was unexpected; it was unnoticed; yet it was and is unsurpassed, and it still remains unfinished.

I

The first Easter was unexpected. Even those who had been with Christ for some three years—those who had such great hopes, those in whose presence the promises had been made—even they did not expect what took place. It is hard to imagine the depths of despair into which the disciples had sunk on that Saturday following the Crucifixion—the day of sorrow and silence. Whether it is an indication of their bravery or whether it merely shows that women were not noticed much, the fact is that the women were the ones who went to the tomb while the men remained in hiding. When they returned from that early-morning visit and reported what they had found, the men dismissed their account as hysterical babbling. That is, all ignored them save two. These two ran to the tomb to see for themselves, not daring to believe at first. All the others rejected the idea. It was so totally unexpected, even to them. They had seen the tomb sealed with the seal of the empire. No one would break that seal, much less roll away the heavy stone.

It was all over. The great dream was finished. This was the end.

One of the great Christian men of our day, C. S. Lewis, has entitled his spiritual autobiography, *Surprised by Joy*.[1] What a fitting phrase for each of us! How often the non-believer, the skeptic, the frustrated person finds himself surprised to discover that there *is* good in the world; that there *is* unexpected promise in our experience when we open our eyes to see. There isn't a one of us who has not seen hopes blasted; who has not seen dreams blighted; who has not had disappointment and frustration. It is easy for us to be depressed and to say, "Oh, what's the use? This is the end." But that which is good in life never ultimately ends, and God cannot be defeated. His purposes may be postponed; his followers may be detoured; but his purpose for good cannot finally be defeated. Jesus once described the kingdom of God as coming as a thief in the night. So often the opportunities for service —and, so often too, the wondrous experience of joy and fullness of life—come unexpectedly. The best things in life so frequently are unexpected. So the first Easter was unexpected.

Often the fullness of Christian experience in our day is unexpected. When we are bowed down beneath a weight too grievous to be borne, from somewhere there comes the vision to see it as a part

[1] (New York: Harcourt, Brace & Company, 1955.)

of God's redemptive purpose. From somewhere the light breaks and the darkness is rolled away. It was —it is—unexpected.

II

The first Easter was unnoticed. What was changed in Jerusalem on that first Easter? Who was changed? Was Herod? So far as we know, he remained the grasping, petty politician he had always been. Was Caiaphas changed, or Annas, his uncle, the power behind the high priest's throne? Not so far as we know. They apparently continued in the same way and were destroyed in A.D. 70. Was Pilate changed? Not so far as we know. We lose sight of Pilate but there are some who have suggested that he fell from favor; that he either committed suicide in his cell, or was executed under Nero. Were the soldiers changed? There is no record, except the legend that served as the basis for Lloyd C. Douglas' book *The Robe*. Was the multitude that had hailed him on Palm Sunday and had shouted "Crucify!" on Friday changed? Not so far as we can tell.

The Resurrection was unnoticed by all, save by those who had had some prior experience with him. Mary Magdalene had been with him; the disciples had been with him; and though there was doubt at first, and amazement, it was to these the meaning of the Resurrection became clear. And only to them!

So it is today. Easter is celebrated around the

85

world, but not in all parts of the world. In the Holy City itself, there are certain keepers of the holy places who allow pilgrims to visit those places on this day, but who do not themselves worship, and who are not themselves affected by that worship—at least, not directly. These are the Moslems who hold that portion of Jesusalem in which the holy places are now located.

For many in our world Easter goes unnoticed. Beneath the joy and wonder and the glory is the sad fact that on many people the resurrection fact seems to have no effect whatsoever. But is not this inevitable? For Easter is not something in and of itself—set apart, detached, out of context; Easter is a part of a whole. It is the climax, yes! But it is the climax of what has gone before.

III

Easter is unsurpassed in glory, hope, joy, wonder. There are some preachers who take advantage of their position in the pulpit to make sarcastic comments about the secular celebration of Easter. This is improper. It is entirely fitting to celebrate with flowers, with new clothes, with various indications of joy the coming of new life into the world in the dawning of the spring. This is a reflection of the part of the wondrous truth of the ongoing creation of God the Father. The secular celebration can be good, valid, and significant as a part of the whole— but only as a part—only as a part which needs to have more added to it. For we must not overlook the Cross.

There would have been no Easter without Good Friday. There can be no resurrection without the Cross. The Celtic cross—the cross with the circle at its center—symbolizes beautifully the oneness of the Atonement and the Resurrection: The cross is empty because it was defeated; the cross has the circle upon it, reminding us of eternal life. Easter, however, is never just the empty, superficial justification of that which has been, without change. It is not the automatic approval of all that has gone before. We miss the point entirely, if we expect to continue unchanged.

Do you enjoy wordplay? If you put the word "immortality" in lower-case letters, the "t" looks like a cross. If you remove that cross from "immortality," you have "immorality." So, if you take the cross—the sacrificial love, the self-sacrificing gift—out of Easter, you end up with something that is fundamentally immoral, for this would imply that Easter was just a glorious way of saying, "Well, everything is O.K. Don't worry about anything any more. There's no obligation to change or to grow in any way; everything is all right." What blasphemy! What a travesty it would be to say to Jesus, "Now you have risen from the tomb; so the suffering on Calvary's hill means nothing. The agony in the garden has no significance whatever. All the teaching and all the striving have no lasting meaning.

87

Everything is just fine the way it has always been!" What blasphemy! Take the cross from immortality and you have immorality.

Easter is unsurpassed in glory because it grows out of self-sacrifice. It comes following the willingness to give. It triumphs over the pain and suffering incidental to love.

After the Second World War an interesting discovery was made in badly blitzed London. Those who examined the bomb craters were amazed to discover flowers growing in these depressions, the like of which had not been seen in London for generations. Botanists could not discover where the flowers had come from. The theory was advanced that the seeds had been buried under the ground in London for generations or even centuries. The buzz bombs coming down and exploding, not only cleared away the covering earth, but also put nitrates into the soil that may have activated these seeds. Life that had been dormant for centuries now came to bloom in beauty in the midst of destruction.

This is not to suggest that in order to have flowers we should bomb a city; nor is it to suggest that one seeks for trouble in order to triumph over it. It is to proclaim that at the center of the Easter fact is the knowledge that God can work for good in all things with those who love him.

We recognize not only that Easter is unsurpassed in glory, but that it is unsurpassed in the frequency of its celebration. We do not celebrate Easter just once a year. We celebrate it formally *every* week. This is the reason Christians celebrate the first day of the week as their day of worship rather than the seventh. We observe Easter fifty-two times a year. But more significantly, we celebrate it every day to the extent that we live strengthened, inspired, led by that faith. And we glory in it every day if we recognize the significance, not of the question, "Is there eternal life?" but of the question, "What is there in my life that is worth being eternal?" For those qualities of life worthy of eternity are eternal.

IV

Easter is unfinished. In some of the most ancient manuscripts, the Gospel according to Mark is not completed. Indeed, in the Revised Standard Version, it is pointed out that some versions end with chapter sixteen, verse eight while others had twelve more verses and still others had but one more verse. If the last page were torn off right in the middle of the Easter account, as one might assume by reading up to verse eight, this becomes something of a parable. The Easter story is not finished. Indeed, it will never be finished until it has been shared with all, and by all—until the fellowship becomes universal.

A preacher was speaking in an open air meeting in London's Hyde Park. Near the platform was a heckler who was dirty and unkempt. After listening for awhile, he interrupted the preacher to say, "Oh, you and your Christianity! What good is it? We've had Christianity for almost two thousand years, and look at the world!" The preacher replied, "Yes, and there has been water available since creation and look at your face!" That's just about it, isn't it? Christianity has not been tried and found wanting. Mankind has been found wanting and Christianity has never been fully tried.

Easter is not just the gift of personal immortality after death; it is the gift of eternal life through all time and eternity. The church, the fellowship of the faithful, the community of those concerned for one another and for all the world, is the resurrected body of Christ, for:

> Christ has no hands but our hands
> To do His work today.[2]

How well are we doing it?

Yes, Easter is unfinished. One of the strangest statements of Jesus is that attributed to him in the Gospel according to John in the Upper Room. In the Upper Room you remember he said to his disciples, "It is to your advantage that I go away" (16:7). How amazing! But think of it this way: *It is to your advantage that my leadership shall not*

[2] Annie Johnson Flint, "The World's Bible." Used by permission of Evangelical Publishers.

*be confined just to my physical presence, but that
the Comforter, the Holy Spirit, the Paraclete, the
Spirit of God shall be known to all of you, and
dwell in you.*

V

Easter was unexpected, unnoticed; is unsurpassed
and unfinished. Note the final verse in the New
Testament lesson: "They were continually . . .
praising and blessing God" (K.J.V.). This can all
be summed up in a meditation penned by one who
has done a great deal in this country with young
people. Percy Hayward wrote:

I showed my friend the empty tomb, so as to prove
to him that the Christ had risen from the dead. I revealed to him the broken seal, and the napkin folded in
a corner. I set before him the written record and many
other infallible proofs that my lord was indeed alive.

But he did not believe. "For," said he, "I have looked
into your heart, and I find it selfish, ambitious and
proud, hot and resentful, envious and grudging. No,
your Christ is dead forevermore!"

Then there came a day when I yearned over my friend
and loved him as my own soul. I forgot my proofs and remembered only his incomparable soul. I forgot my proofs
and remembered only his incomparable need. I gave
up mine argument and merely stretched forth mine hand
with an aching tenderness in its touch. I became so concerned for his plan that somehow my own was forgotten
and failed, and I did not care. I sought out the bruises

91

that life had left upon his soul, and in some strange fashion I became a minister for their healing.

And then he believed! "For," said he, "I have seen the living Christ walking in the world. I know. *I know* that he indeed is risen from the dead and become the first fruits of them that sleep in the charnel house of self. Yea, your Christ liveth." [3]

"Thanks be to God, who gives us the victory through our Lord Jesus Christ. Therefore, . . . be steadfast, immovable, always abounding in the work of the Lord, knowing that in the Lord your labor is not in vain."

---

[3] Used by permission of Josephine L. Hayward.